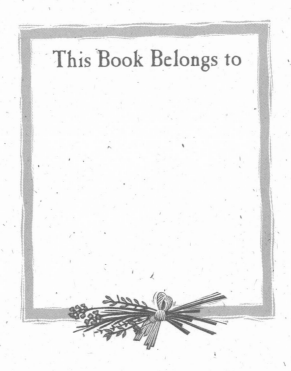

This Book Belongs to

*The mission of Storey Communications is to serve our customers
by publishing practical information that encourages personal independence
in harmony with the environment.*

Edited by Pamela Lappies
Cover and interior illustrations by Mary Rich
Design and production by Meredith Maker
Production assistance by Susan Bernier
Indexed by Northwind Editorial Services

Some recipes have been adapted from other Storey Publishing books: pages 6, 10, 24, 33: *The Pleasure of Herbs* by Phyllis Shaudys; pages 8, 12: *Herbs for Weddings* by Bertha Reppert; pages 20, 34, 36, 38, 60: *At Home with Herbs* by Jane Newdick; page 42: *Growing & Using Scented Geraniums* by Mary Peddie, Judy Lewis, and John Lewis; pages 48, 50: *Herbal Vinegar* by Maggie Oster; pages 56, 58: *Jams, Jellies & Preserves* by Imogene McTague.

Printed in Canada by Métropole Litho

10 9 8 7 6 5 4 3 2 1

**Library of Congress
Cataloging-in-Publication Data**

Bass, Ruth, 1934–
    Herbal sweets / Ruth Bass.
        p.   cm.
    "A fresh-from-the-garden cookbook."
    "A Storey Publishing Book."
    ISBN 0-88266-922-2 (hc : alk paper)
    1. Cookery (Herbs)   2. Desserts.
        I. Title.
TX819.H4B75 1996
641.6'57—dc20   95-53967
                                                    CIP

HeRBAL SWeeTS

A
Fresh from the Garden
Cookbook

RUTH BASS

ILLUSTRATED BY MARY RICH

STOREY

A Storey Publishing Book

Storey Communications, Inc.

Introduction

To heal, to beautify, to flavor, to decorate — herbs have been at the core of most cultures throughout history. The Chinese and the Greeks developed medicinal drugs from herbs; the Romans made the culinary properties of these fragrant, pungent plants part of their civilization; and in medieval monasteries, the garden near the kitchen and the infirmary was a source for both food and well-being. In the 16th and 17th centuries, people became aware that a container of dried herbs and rose petals could help banish some of the unpleasant smells of daily living. Potpourris became commonplace, sachets were made to freshen clothes-storage areas, and sweet waters made from lavender and roses were sprinkled about in residences.

Whether it was the fancy knot gardens, filled with painstakingly pruned herbs on the grounds of the English castles, or the practical kitchen gardens outside the crude houses of the first settlement at Plymouth, herbs have held a place in human history for thousands of years.

In soups and salads, they are ubiquitous. With chicken, beef, and pork, they make an impact. They have entered the bread world with subtlety, and they adorn many vegetables. Their use in sweets is less common, although Victorian cooks often used herbs to flavor sweet dishes, and medieval cooks did not limit use of herbs to particular courses at a feast.

The best incentive for using herbs comes from having them at hand. As one contemporary chef said, "When the herbs are growing outside the kitchen door, you start using them." If you have tarragon, borage, lemon thyme, and lemon verbena right there, you'll reach for them. Just as you substitute a fruit or vegetable in a recipe because it's ripe, it looks good, or it's on sale, you'll find yourself reaching for oregano instead of basil, cilantro instead of parsley, savory instead of marjoram.

Suddenly herbs have jumped out of the salad dressing and into the ice cream. Or chilled drinks. Or cakes and sorbets.

Those who live in deserts — concrete or sand and rock — need not despair at this talk of kitchen gardens and fresh-picked herbs. Supermarkets are savvy about herbs now, and it's not just parsley that cozies up to the broccoli and green beans. At the best stores you'll find lots of herbs, often in plastic packets, crisp and green. Many herbs will grow inside your city apartment or air-conditioned Southwestern home: They take well to pots and windowsills.

This collection is intended to start the adventurous cook on his or her way. It provides tasty chutneys, interesting punches and alcoholic drinks, pretty garnishes, and unusual ice creams, cakes, and cookies. The hope is that a frosted lavender flower or rose-petal ice cream will set off a flurry of creativity that will make parsley, sage, rosemary, and thyme regular members of the cast for curtain-call dishes.

A word of caution: If you have planned a heavily herbed soup, or you're serving a chicken dish doused in oregano, you might want to steer clear of thyme sorbet or anise cookies. Too much enthusiasm may frazzle the palate.

5

Old-Fashioned Herbed Candies

Penny candies in the old-fashioned general store were often made with combinations of herbs, and some tasted more hot than sweet, more bitter than refreshing. Here's a recipe that can be adapted to fit everyone's taste.

Herbs to try include peppermint, horehound, spearmint, orangemint, applemint, wintergreen, lemon verbena, and lemon catnip. For variation, add 1 tablespoon mint leaves or 1 teaspoon crushed anise seeds to horehound for a horehound candy.

> 4 cups boiling water
> 2 cups herb leaves with stems and blossoms
> 3 cups granulated sugar
> 3 cups brown sugar
> ½ tablespoon butter

1. Pour boiling water over the leaves and steep for 10 minutes, longer for stronger tea. Meanwhile, butter a shallow pan.
2. Strain the leaves, add the sugar and butter to the tea, and bring it to a boil over medium heat. Continue boiling until syrup hardens when a small amount is dropped into cold water.
3. Pour into the buttered pan and score the candy into squares before it sets, or break it up into pieces as soon as it hardens. Wrap each hardened piece in waxed paper. Store in an airtight container.

Frosted Lavender Sticks

The somewhat floppy, gray-green lavender leaves and purple flowers create a soft corner in the herb garden. Sugared, the flowers are a crisply pretty nibble. You should be sure the plants have not been sprayed with herbicides or pesticides. For variety, substitute violets or rose petals for the lavender.

> 12 stalks fresh lavender flowers
> 1 egg white, beaten until frothy
> ½ cup granulated sugar

1. Dip the flowers of the lavender stalks in egg white, then roll in or dust with sugar. If you are worried about eating uncooked egg whites, substitute the proper amount of pasteurized, dried egg whites, which are available in most supermarkets.
2. Air dry on waxed paper.

1 DOZEN STICKS

Sweet Lemon Bars

Sweet lemon may be an oxymoron, but it works. These sugary confections, flavored with lemon juice and lemon thyme, tempt the palate with their sweet-tart taste.

¼ cup confectioners' sugar
½ cup butter
1 cup unbleached flour, sifted
2 eggs
1 cup granulated sugar
½ teaspoon baking powder
¼ teaspoon salt
Juice of 1 large lemon
1 teaspoon fresh minced lemon thyme or ½ teaspoon dried

1. Preheat the oven to 350°F. Cream the butter and sugar. Add the sifted flour, blending smoothly. Using your fingers, press the mixture into an 8 x 8-inch pan. Bake 20 minutes.
2. Beat together the eggs, sugar, baking powder, salt, lemon juice, and lemon thyme. Pour over the crust and bake another 20 minutes.
3. Cool, then cut into squares.

16 BARS

Lemon Thyme Cookies

When time is a problem, cookies that can be made over two days may help with the daily race against the clock. These have the fragrance of thyme as well, in this case lemon thyme, just one of some 350 species of this perennial, which often works nicely as a decorative plant in a rock or container garden. If lemon thyme is hard to come by, substitute one of the others.

> 1 cup butter or margarine, softened
> 1½ cups granulated sugar
> 2 eggs
> 2½ cups unbleached flour
> 1 teaspoon cream of tartar
> ½ teaspoon salt
> 5 tablespoons finely chopped fresh lemon thyme or
>   3 tablespoons dried

1. Cream the butter with the sugar, add the eggs, and mix well.
2. Sift together the flour, cream of tartar, and salt. Stir the flour mixture into the butter, sugar, and eggs until well blended, then add the lemon thyme.
3. Chill overnight or until firm enough to roll.
4. Preheat the oven to 350°F. Roll the chilled dough into 1-inch balls and bake on a greased cookie sheet for 10 minutes.

4 DOZEN COOKIES

Thyme was once thought to relieve
epilepsy and melancholy.

11

Crisp Caraway Cookies

Caraway seeds bring a distinctive taste to many breads, cakes, and cookies, especially in the cuisine of northern and eastern Europe. The leaves of the plant are mild tasting, usually used in soups, but less common than the crunchy seeds. For a different taste, substitute poppy seeds here.

1⅔ cups unbleached flour
1 teaspoon baking powder
¼ teaspoon baking soda
¼ teaspoon salt
2 teaspoons caraway seeds
½ cup butter or margarine, softened
⅔ cup granulated sugar
2 eggs
½ teaspoon vanilla extract

1. Preheat the oven to 375°F.
2. Mix together flour, baking powder, baking soda, salt, and caraway seeds. Set aside.
3. Cream the butter and sugar until fluffy. Add the eggs and vanilla, and beat well.

4. Stir in the flour mixture. Wrap the dough in plastic wrap and chill several hours, overnight, or until firm enough to roll (the dough will still be rather soft).

5. Cut the dough into quarters. Work with one quarter at a time, keeping the rest in the refrigerator. Roll the dough very thin on a floured surface. (Use a pastry cloth and covered rolling pin to prevent the dough from sticking.) Cut with a floured 3-inch round cutter. Put on ungreased cookie sheets.

6. Bake on the top rack of oven 8 to 10 minutes, watching closely. Remove to a wire rack to cool. Repeat until the dough is gone. Store in an airtight container or freezer.

4 DOZEN COOKIES

According to folklore, caraway has the power to cure hysterics and to keep lovers true.

Anise Bars

A licoricelike flavor emanates from anise, which is actually a member of the parsley family. From its small yellowish-white flowers come anise seeds and oil. (If you can't find anise oil, you can make your own by combining a tablespoon of anise seeds with a half cup of salad oil in a sterilized bottle and letting the mixture stand in the refrigerator for a week before using. For a stronger flavor, just increase the proportion of anise seeds.)

2 cups unbleached flour
1 teaspoon baking powder
¾ cup granulated sugar
¼ cup butter
2 eggs, beaten
1½ drops anise oil
1 teaspoon anise seeds
¼ cup butter or margarine, melted

1. Preheat the oven to 375°F.
2. In a food processor, blend flour, baking powder, and sugar. Cut butter into half-inch chunks and add to the flour mixture. Blend briefly. The mixture will not be smooth. Add the eggs and anise oil, and blend for two seconds or until smooth.

3. Cut the dough in half. Roll out one piece to ¼-inch thick and then cut into sticks, about 3½-inches long and ½-inch wide. If you use a zigzag cutter, you'll get a pretty, crimped edge. Place the bars on ungreased baking sheets.
4. Add the anise seeds to the melted butter or margarine, and brush on lightly with a pastry brush. Bake 10 minutes and cool on a rack.

2 DOZEN BARS

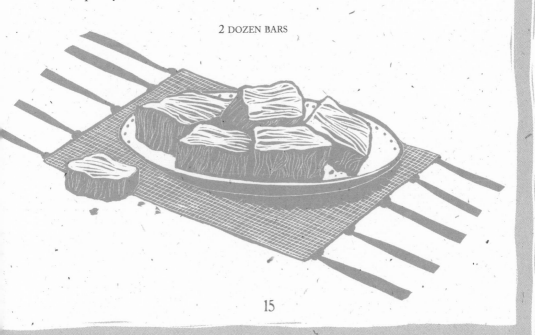

Shortbread Cookies with Thyme

"Parsley, sage, rosemary and thyme," sang Simon and Garfunkel, flavoring the music of a generation. Just two of their four herbs create rich harmony here. If you use dried herbs, use half as much.

> ½ cup plus 1 tablespoon butter
> ¼ cup confectioners' sugar
> 1½ cups flour
> 1 teaspoon lemon zest
> 2 teaspoons minced fresh rosemary
> 2 teaspoons minced fresh thyme
> Extra confectioners' sugar

1. Cream the butter and sugar together by hand or in a food processor. Add the flour, lemon zest, rosemary, and thyme. Knead gently to make a soft dough and chill for an hour.
2. Preheat the oven to 350°F. Roll the dough on a pastry cloth or lightly floured surface about ⅜-inch thick, and cut into diamonds, circles, or free forms. Pinching the edges, pie fashion, will create an attractive crinkle.

3. Place the cookies on a greased cookie sheet. Bake for 15 to 20 minutes or until the cookies are lightly golden. It is important not to overbake.
4. Sprinkle lightly with the extra confectioners' sugar while the cookies are hot. Cool on a rack.

2–3 DOZEN COOKIES, DEPENDING ON THE CUTS

Pungent Minty Tea

This tea, an old-fashioned recipe, lets the mint bite. Delicious served hot, it also makes a wonderfully refreshing iced tea.

> *3 tablespoons tea leaves*
> *4 cups boiling water*
> *½ cup freshly chopped mint leaves*

1. Pour the boiling water over the tea leaves and steep until it reaches desired strength. Strain.
2. Pour the hot tea over the mint leaves and steep 1 minute. Strain and serve. For iced tea, let cool and pour over ice cubes.

2 SERVINGS

Grandma's Iced Tea

When the scent of fresh-mown hay comes from the fields, and July days are hot and humid, a tall glass of this tea, served with lunch or in the shade of an old tree by the pond, cools the palate. It's also good while you're relaxing in a wicker loveseat on the porch.

> 5 *teaspoons orange pekoe tea*
> 10 *heaping tablespoons granulated sugar*
> 2 *tablespoons chopped fresh spearmint*
> *Juice and rind of one orange*
> *Juice and rind of one lemon*
> 4 *cups boiling water*
> *Cold water*

1. Put the tea in a strainer and pour boiling water over it into the sugar, spearmint, and fruit juice and rinds. Keep dipping the strainer into the liquid until it is a medium brown color.
2. Add enough cold water to make 2 quarts. Remove the fruit rinds before serving.

2 QUARTS

Peppermint Angel Food Cake

Angel food cake is an American favorite. This one has a peppermint twist. For a special occasion, serve with peppermint stick ice cream and a spot of chocolate sauce. Or serve it plain, garnished with a sprig of fresh mint.

1 cup cake flour
2 tablespoons cornstarch
¾ cup granulated sugar
5 large egg whites
½ teaspoon vanilla extract
1 tablespoon finely chopped fresh peppermint

1. Preheat the oven to 350°F. Use nonstick baking paper to line the base of an ungreased angel food cake pan.
2. Sift together the flour, the cornstarch, and 1 tablespoon of the sugar.
3. Beat the egg whites until stiff. Use a whisk to gradually add the rest of the sugar, continuing to whisk the mixture until very thick.
4. Fold in the flour mixture, vanilla, and mint. Turn into the pan and bake 35 to 40 minutes.
5. Invert the cake, still in the pan, over a tray of ice cubes to cool. Do not unmold until cold. Serve drizzled with Minted Chocolate Sauce, if desired (page 22).

6 SERVINGS

Black-stemmed peppermint has the strongest flavor.

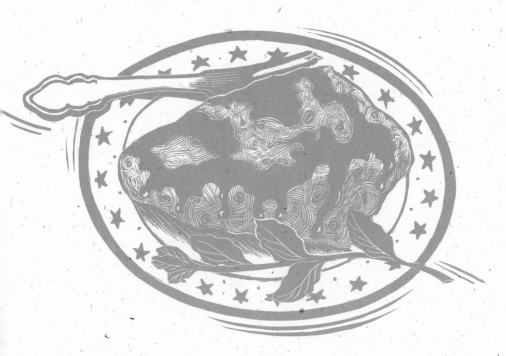

Minted Chocolate Sauce

To put a little zip into traditional chocolate sauce, add a little mint. The quick way is to add a few drops of peppermint extract to the chocolate sauce. Only slightly longer to prepare is the following sauce made with fresh mint.

> ½ cup water
> ½ cup coarsely chopped fresh mint leaves, crushed
> 3 squares unsweetened chocolate
> ¾ cup sugar
> ¼ teaspoon salt
> 4½ tablespoons butter or margarine
> ½ teaspoon vanilla extract
> ½ cup water

1. Boil ¼ cup of the water and pour over the mint leaves in a small bowl. Let stand for 10 minutes.
2. In a small saucepan, melt the chocolate in the other ¼ cup of water. (Or combine and heat in the microwave oven about 2 minutes, stirring after 1 minute.)

3. Strain the mint-flavored water into a small saucepan with the melted chocolate, sugar, and salt. Cook, stirring, about 5 minutes or until the sugar melts and the mixture thickens.

4. Stir in the butter and vanilla, and continue heating until the butter melts. Serve hot or cold.

1¼ CUPS

*Mints have been used medicinally
for more than 5,000 years.*

Lemon Cheesecake

Calendulas are an intrepid summer annual, brightly coloring the garden through rain, drought, heat, and even the coolness of fall. Sometimes called pot marigold, calendula is often used as a way to add color to cheese or cakes — even to fabric. Finely ground calendula petals can be added to this cheesecake for color and a few petals or blossoms used as a garnish on each serving.

6 eggs, separated
½ cup plus 2 tablespoons butter
½ cup plus 2 tablespoons sugar
12 ounces softened cream cheese
4 teaspoons chopped fresh lemon balm or 2 teaspoons dried
4 teaspoons lemon zest
2 teaspoons finely ground calendula petals (optional)

*In the language of flowers,
lemon balm stands for sympathy.*

1. Preheat the oven to 325°F.
2. In a small mixer bowl, beat the egg whites until they stand in soft peaks.
3. In another bowl, cream the butter, sugar, egg yolks, and cream cheese. Add the lemon balm, lemon zest, and petals to the butter mixture. Fold in the beaten egg whites.
4. Place in a greased angel food tube pan and bake 55 minutes. Cool 10 minutes before inverting on plate.

10 SERVINGS

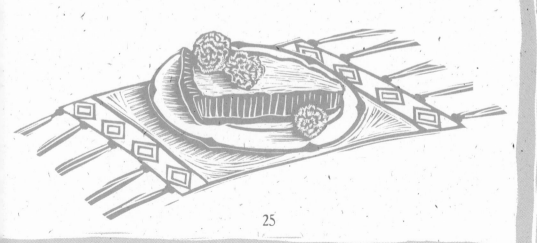

Maple Sage Apple Cake

Usually you put maple syrup on your pancakes and sage in the Thanksgiving turkey stuffing. This time they are teamed up in a beautiful, dark cake made in a shaped pan lined with apple slices and flavored with applesauce. For the full taste, use real maple syrup — blends don't have the same effect.

MAPLE SAGE APPLESAUCE

3 or 4 tart, crisp apples
2 tablespoons maple syrup
2 sage leaves
1 tablespoon water
Juice of half a lemon

1. Peel, core, and cut-up the apples. Combine them with the syrup and sage leaves in a small saucepan. Add a tablespoon or so of water to prevent sticking.
2. Keep the heat low and cook until the apples are soft. Remove the sage, add the lemon juice, and whip with a wire whisk until smooth.

26

Maple Sage Apple Cake

⅞ cup butter
2 cups unbleached flour
1 teaspoon baking soda
1 teaspoon baking powder
½ teaspoon salt
1 teaspoon cinnamon
1 cup plus 4 tablespoons packed
   dark brown sugar

2 eggs
1 tablespoon minced fresh sage
1 cup Maple Sage Applesauce
2 large apples, Cortland, Mutsu, or
   Spy, peeled, quartered, and cored
Juice of half a lemon

1. Preheat the oven to 350°F. Use 2 tablespoons of the butter to generously grease the bottom and sides of a 9½-inch bundt pan.
2. Sift the flour with the baking soda, baking powder, salt, and cinnamon.
3. Cream 1 cup of the brown sugar and the remainder of the butter, or combine quickly in a food processor. Blend in the eggs. Add the minced sage and the Maple Sage Applesauce to the sugar mixture and process or beat well.
4. Gradually add the flour mixture to the applesauce mixture, blending well.
5. Slice the apples thinly and toss with the lemon juice. Sprinkle the extra 4 tablespoons of brown sugar over the buttered surfaces of the bundt pan and arrange the apple slices around the bottom and sides of the pan.
6. Pour the batter into the pan, taking care not to disturb the apple slices. Bake 50 to 60 minutes, until the top is golden brown and a cake tester or toothpick comes out clean. Cool to room temperature on a rack before taking the cake out of the pan. Loosen, then invert the glossy cake on a plate.

8–10 SERVINGS

Lemon Sponge with Rosemary

This classy dessert combines the sharpness of lemon with rosemary, the herb that makes noses wiggle in the kitchen and insists on being noticed in any dish. Be sure to remove all the stems and to mince the rosemary as finely as possible. It's a tough-leaved herb, and while it's traditionally associated with remembrance, it ought to be as subtle as possible here.

> 1 cup sugar
> 3 tablespoons flour
> 2 eggs, separated
> Juice and zest of a large lemon
> 1 tablespoon melted butter or margarine
> ⅛ teaspoon salt
> 1 teaspoon finely chopped fresh rosemary
> 1 cup milk
> Rosemary sprigs for garnish

1. Heat the oven to 350°F.
2. Mix the sugar and flour. Beat the egg yolks and add them, along with the lemon juice and zest, butter, salt, and rosemary, to the sugar and flour.
3. Stir in the milk. Beat the egg whites until they stand in soft peaks, and add to the mixture.

4. Pour into a casserole dish or into individual custard cups. Set in a large pan containing an inch of hot water and bake for 30 to 40 minutes. The top should be slightly browned. Additional rosemary sprigs may be used for garnish.

6 SERVINGS

Raspberry Peach Tart

Ever since someone invented Peach Melba, the world has known that raspberries and peaches are a fit. In this case, they are equal partners, housed in a crunchy graham cracker crust.

> 3 *medium fresh peaches*
> ¼ *teaspoon lemon juice*
> 1 *cup fresh raspberries*
> 2 *cups plain yogurt*
> 4 *tablespoons confectioners' sugar*
> 2 *teaspoons chopped fresh mint*
> 9-inch *graham cracker crust*
> 2 *teaspoons granulated sugar*

1. Coarsely chop 2 peaches and sprinkle with lemon juice to keep them from turning brown. Gently wash the raspberries and combine with the peaches.
2. Stir half the yogurt, sugar, and mint together and spread in the 9-inch graham cracker crust. Arrange the fruit over the yogurt mixture, cover with plastic wrap, and refrigerate for an hour.

3. Just before serving, stir the 2 teaspoons of sugar into the rest of the yogurt and put a dollop on each section of the tart. Slice the remaining peach and arrange on top to garnish.

6 SERVINGS

Tangerine Cooler

Sweet tangerines, lime-green kiwis with their distinctive black seeds, bananas, and orange juice blend in a fruit drink that will cut the thirst created by a summer day.

> 2 tangerines, peeled, sectioned, and trimmed
> 2 ripe kiwifruit, peeled and sliced
> 2 bananas, peeled and sliced
> 1 cup orange juice
> 2 tablespoons chopped fresh mint, plus four sprigs
>   for garnish
> Crushed ice

1. Chill four tall glasses in the freezer.
2. In a blender, combine the tangerines, kiwifruit, bananas, orange juice, and chopped mint. Puree.
3. Fill the chilled glasses with crushed ice and add the fruit mixture. Garnish each drink with a mint sprig and serve.

4 SERVINGS

Rosemary Fruit Punch

Herbs put both fragrance and punch into the punch. For a delicious golden brew, try this — either well-chilled for summer or hot for a fireside party in the winter.

> 1 can pineapple juice (46 ounces)
> 5 sprigs fresh rosemary or 1 tablespoon dried
> ½ cup sugar
> Juice of 8 lemons (about 1½ cups)
> 1½ cups cranberry juice
> 2 cups water
> 1 quart ginger ale
> Paper-thin lemon slices for garnish

1. In a small saucepan, heat 1 cup of pineapple juice until it boils. Remove from heat, add the rosemary, and steep 8 to 10 minutes.
2. Dissolve the sugar in the hot juice and then strain into a pitcher containing the remaining pineapple juice, lemon juice, cranberry juice, and water. Chill, if serving cold.
3. Just before serving, add the ginger ale and garnish with the lemon slices.

3¾ QUARTS

Lavender Ice Cream

In fiction, lavender goes with old lace, and in ice cream, it exudes elegance as well. This ice cream, from Jane Newdick's *At Home with Herbs*, is easy to make and should be served with miniature macaroons or vanilla wafers. Flower heads, of course, must be unsprayed.

> *4 egg yolks*
> *¾ cup sugar*
> *⅔ cup half-and-half*
> *6 fresh lavender flower heads*
> *⅔ cup whipping or heavy cream*

1. Whisk the egg yolks and sugar together until light and foamy. In a saucepan, gently heat the half-and-half with the lavender flowers. Bring to a boil, then strain into the egg yolk mixture.
2. Return the mixture to the stove and cook over very low heat, stirring constantly until it is slightly thickened and coats the back of a spoon. Do not let it boil. Pour the custard into a bowl, and refrigerate until it is really cold.

3. Whip the cream until it forms peaks. Fold into the cold custard. Process in an ice-cream maker or freeze in a container.

4 SERVINGS

Lemon Thyme Sorbet

Thyme, examined closely, has the tiniest of leaves and shrubby little stems.
In fact, it's sometimes called a shrublet. So make sure it's just the leaves you're
chopping, not the stalks, when you're adding this lemony herb to what could be
a perfect entremets — this palate-clearing sorbet.

> ½ cup sugar
> 1½ cups water
> Juice and thinly pared rinds of two lemons
> 4 tablespoons fresh lemon thyme leaves
> 1 egg white or an equal amount of pasteurized,
>   dried egg whites

1. Heat the sugar, water, and lemon rinds in a heavy-bottomed saucepan, allowing the sugar to dissolve without stirring. If crystals start to form on the sides of the pan, brush them down into the liquid with a wet pastry brush.
2. Bring to a boil and boil briskly for 5 minutes. Remove the pan from the heat, and dip the base briefly in cold water to stop the cooking process. Add the thyme leaves to the syrup and let cool completely.
3. When cooled, strain off the leaves and rinds and add the lemon juice. Process in an ice-cream freezer. When the mixture is nearly frozen, beat the egg white until it stands in soft peaks and add to the mixture for a sorbet with a smooth texture.

4 SERVINGS

Rose Petal Ice Cream

For delicacy, the shell-pink color of this ice cream and its faint scent of roses are an unbeatable combination. Serve it in a tall sherbet glass or fluted pastry shell. Use highly scented red rose petals from a plant that has not been sprayed with pesticides or herbicides.

1 cup whipping cream
1 cup half-and-half
Petals of 4 scented roses
2 egg yolks
¾ cup sugar
¼ teaspoon vanilla extract
2 teaspoons honey

1. In a saucepan, heat the cream, half-and-half, and rose petals almost to the boiling point, removing from the heat just before the mixture boils. Cover and let sit until cool.
2. In a large mixing bowl, whisk together egg yolks, sugar, vanilla, and honey until creamy. Strain the rose-flavored cream mixture into the egg mixture and stir. Pour into a double boiler and cook until slightly thickened, but do not let it boil.

3. Chill the custard mixture, then freeze it or process it in an ice-cream maker. Store in the freezer. Let it soften about 20 minutes before serving.

4–6 SERVINGS

Lime-Mint Sherbet

For a refreshing dessert, topped perhaps with a bit of Minted Chocolate
Sauce (page 22), try this sherbet. Hint: The rinds of lemons and limes can
be harvested easily for zest if you get a small tool called a lemon zester from
your kitchenware shop.

> 12 sprigs fresh mint
> 2 cups water
> ¾ cup granulated sugar
> ½ cup light corn syrup
> 2 teaspoons lime zest
> Juice of 4 limes
> 2 egg whites

1. Set the freezer control for fast freezing.
2. Remove the stems from the mint leaves and chop fine. In a saucepan,
   combine the mint leaves, water, and sugar. Bring to a boil, stirring until
   sugar dissolves. Cool.

3. Strain the cooled mixture. Add the corn syrup, lime zest, and juice. Freeze until firm.
4. Break up the mixture and beat to a smooth mush. Beat the egg whites until they stand in soft peaks. Fold into mixture and freeze until firm.

2 PINTS

Rose Geranium Syrup

Another interesting sauce for ice cream — or as a marinade for fruits — is this flowery syrup, which can be made ahead of time and stored in sterilized jars.

> 2½ *cups water*
> 2 *cups sugar*
> 1 *handful rose geranium leaves*

1. Place the water and sugar in a deep saucepan, and stir until dissolved.
2. Heat to a boil and let boil for 5 minutes without stirring. Remove from heat, add the rose geranium leaves, cover, and steep for 10 minutes.
3. Strain the syrup into a clean pan and boil for 30 seconds. Remove from heat. Pour into jars that have been sterilized. The syrup keeps 6 to 9 months in the refrigerator.

4–5 HALF-PINT JARS

In the language of flowers,
rose geranium represents "preference."

Blueberries Romanoff

When you serve this, you may catch your guests licking their spoons or their fingers. Easily doubled or tripled for a buffet, this melt-in-your-mouth dessert tastes and looks delicious.

> *2 pints fresh blueberries*
> *1 cup confectioners' sugar*
> *1 cup whipping cream*
> *2 teaspoons minced fresh mint*
> *2 tablespoons orange liqueur*

1. Gently rinse the blueberries with cold water. Drain. Place them in a medium-size glass bowl, sprinkle with sugar, and mix, taking care not to crush the berries. Refrigerate for an hour, stirring occasionally.
2. Whip the cream until stiff, adding the minced mint and the liqueur. Fold the cream into the blueberries. Serve at once.

6 SERVINGS

Fruit Bowl

A hearty or especially spicy dinner calls for a light hand with the dessert. Try this refreshing mixed fruit bowl with Lemon Thyme Cookies (page 10) or gingersnaps for a perfect ending. The fruits can be varied with the season, with little chance of putting in the "wrong" one.

1 pint raspberries, fresh or frozen
1 ripe honeydew melon, scooped into balls
1 ripe cantaloupe, scooped into balls
1 pint sliced peaches, fresh or frozen
1 sweet orange, cut into chunks
1 grapefruit, cut into chunks
1 pint halved strawberries, fresh or frozen
1 pint fresh blueberries, if available
2 tablespoons finely chopped fresh mint or 1 teaspoon dried
1 tablespoon finely chopped fresh lemon balm
Sugar to taste (start with ½ cup)
2 ounces Cointreau or other orange-based liqueur
1 banana, sliced
1 kiwifruit, sliced

1. Place the raspberries, melon balls, peaches, orange chunks, grapefruit chunks, strawberries, and blueberries in a large, decorative glass bowl. Gently toss with the mint, lemon balm, sugar, and liqueur. Refrigerate for an hour or more.
2. The citrus will keep the peaches from discoloring, but you'll still want to add the banana slices just before serving. Decorate with the black-seeded kiwifruit.

8–12 SERVINGS

Rosemary Pears

The delicacy of pears is enhanced by an almost candied taste and the fragrance of rosemary. The pears should be ripe but still firm so they will hold their shape in the cooking.

3 *ripe pears*
Zest of half a lemon
½ *teaspoon finely chopped rosemary*
1½ *tablespoons sugar*
1 *tablespoon butter*
½ *cup dry white wine*
3 *tablespoons brandy*

1. Preheat the oven to 300°F.
2. Cut the unpeeled pears lengthwise, removing the blossom and stem ends and scooping out the seeds with a melon baller. With foil, line a casserole that will hold the pears in a single layer.
3. Set the pears in the dish, skin side down. Sprinkle lemon zest, then rosemary and sugar over the pears, and dot with butter. Pour wine into the bottom of the casserole.
4. Bake until the pears are cooked but not soft, about 15 minutes, depending on the pears. Then place the pears under the broiler until the sugar turns slightly brown. Spoon the brandy into the seed cavities, light with a match, and let burn for about a minute.

6 SERVINGS

*In early times, rosemary was
an emblem of fidelity.*

Peach-Plum Chutney

The gold of peaches, yellow plums, mustard seed, and turmeric characterizes this tasty chutney, a tangy offset for the mild flavor of poached or baked fish or chicken.

CINNAMON BASIL WHITE WINE VINEGAR
> 2 *tablespoons ground cinnamon*
> 2 *tablespoons white wine vinegar*
> 2 *cups basil leaves*

1. Tie the cinnamon in a square of muslin or cheesecloth. Put the vinegar in a stainless steel saucepan and add the cinnamon. Heat the mixture to 110°F. Remove the pan from the heat and let the vinegar cool slightly. Pour into a container for steeping.
2. Remove the stems from the basil leaves and add the leaves to the vinegar. Cover the container tightly and set in a dark place at room temperature. Shake the container every few days. Check the flavor after a week. If the flavor is not strong enough, let it continue to set for up to a month.
3. Strain the vinegar, put it in a storage container, and seal tightly.

Peach-Plum Chutney

1½ pounds freestone peaches, pitted and chopped

1½ pounds yellow plums, pitted and chopped

1 cup chopped white onion

1 sweet yellow pepper, cored, seeded, and chopped

2 tablespoons fresh minced ginger

1 garlic clove, minced

1 fresh green or red hot pepper, seeded and minced

2 cups packed light brown sugar

1 cup cinnamon basil white wine vinegar

½ cup fresh cinnamon basil, minced

1 tablespoon fresh lemon zest

1 teaspoon mustard seeds

1 teaspoon ground cloves

1 teaspoon ground cinnamon

½ teaspoon ground coriander seeds

½ teaspoon turmeric

2 teaspoons non-iodized salt

1. Using a food processor, chop the fruits and vegetables. Combine all ingredients in an 8-quart heavy-bottomed pot. Bring to a boil, stirring constantly. Reduce the heat and simmer for 20 minutes, stirring often.
2. Pour into hot half-pint jars with two-piece canning lids and process by the boiling water bath method (jars on a rack, submerged in boiling water) for 15 minutes.

6 HALF-PINT JARS

Rhubarb Chutney

In springtime, when rhubarb sprouts its crisp red stalks, the simmering of this colorful and spicy chutney will send a delightful aroma through the house. Preserved, it can be enjoyed all year as a condiment with rice and meats.

1 cup dried cherries
7 cups chopped rhubarb
1 cup red onion, chopped
1½ cups apple, cored and chopped
3 garlic cloves, minced
1 tablespoon minced fresh ginger
½ cup minced fresh lovage
2 cups packed light brown sugar
1 cup red wine vinegar
1 teaspoon each of ground cinnamon, cloves, allspice,
    and coriander seeds

1. Combine all ingredients in an 8-quart heavy-bottomed pot. Stirring constantly, heat until boiling.
2. Reduce heat and simmer about 30 minutes, stirring often. Pour into hot half-pint jars with two-piece canning lids and process by the boiling water bath method (jars on a rack, submerged in boiling water) for 15 minutes.

6 HALF-PINT JARS

Herb Crabapple Jelly

Herbs blend wonderfully with apples and crabapples. If you can find cooking crabapples (the ones from the decorative trees are not the same), the jelly will have a glorious rosy color. Apples have enough natural pectin to make jelly on their own.

> 2 cups apple juice
> ½ cup mint, basil thyme, lemon verbena,
>   rose geranium, or tarragon leaves
> ¾ cup granulated sugar

1. Combine ingredients in saucepan. Heat until sugar dissolves and mixture has jelled, about 30 minutes.
2. Pour into hot, sterilized canning jars with two-piece lids, leaving a ¼-inch headspace. Process 5 minutes in a boiling water bath (place jars on a rack in a deep kettle and cover with water until about ¼-inch over lids).

2 HALF-PINT JARS

Minted Wine Jelly

Muscatel, product of the muscat grape, is a sweet dessert wine with a gold or amber color. Add one of the mints and you'll have a flavorful replacement for the traditional apple mint jelly.

>2 cups muscatel
>3 cups sugar
>½ bottle liquid fruit pectin
>3 tablespoons chopped fresh mint leaves
>Sprigs of fresh mint

1. In the top of a double boiler, cook the wine and sugar over rapidly boiling water, stirring constantly. It will take about 2 minutes for the sugar to dissolve.
2. Remove top of double boiler from heat, stir in the pectin, and add the mint.
3. Place a sprig of mint in each sterilized, half-pint glass jar (with two-piece canning lids). Seal at once, and store in a cool place.

4 HALF-PINT JARS

Herb Jellies

Piquant jellies can be made with any number of fresh herbs: basil, lemon verbena, marjoram, mint, parsley, rosemary, sage, tarragon, or thyme. This basic recipe can be used for any one of them, or they can be combined. Rosemary and tarragon, for instance, live together nicely, as do basil and parsley. Sage and cilantro, on the other hand, would clash.

> 1 cup fresh herbs, leaves and stems, plus 10 leaves for garnish
> 2½ cups boiling water
> 4½ cups granulated sugar
> ¼ cup lemon juice or vinegar
> ½ bottle liquid pectin

1. In a saucepan, pour the boiling water over the herbs, cover, and let stand for 20 minutes.
2. Add sugar and lemon juice to the infusion. Heat until sugar dissolves. Bring mixture to a boil and add pectin. Boil for 1 minute, stirring constantly.
3. Remove from heat and skim off the foam. Place a few fresh herb leaves into each jelly jar. Pour into jars with two-piece canning lids and process 5 minutes in a boiling hot water bath with jars submerged.

4 HALF-PINT JARS

If the day and the night are such
that you greet them with joy,
and life emits a fragrance like flowers
and sweet-scented herbs . . . that is your success.

—Henry David Thoreau

Tomato Herb Jelly

In September, when the garden is too full of tomatoes and the air is pretty clear of humidity, the time is right for making jams and jellies. This combination of tomatoes and herbs has a dash of hotness and will make an excellent condiment to serve with meat or chicken dishes. It will taste good on toast, as well.

¼ cup chopped fresh sage or crushed fresh marjoram
¼ cup crushed fresh thyme
1 cup water
1 cup tomato juice
Dash of Tabasco or other hot, red sauce
Juice of 3 lemons, strained (about ½ cup)
2 cups honey
2 cups granulated sugar
6 ounces liquid pectin

1. In a small saucepan, combine the herbs with the water. Simmer gently for 5 minutes. Remove from heat and let stand for 30 minutes.
2. In a large stainless-steel or enameled pot, combine the tomato juice, hot sauce, lemon juice, honey, and sugar. Strain the herbs. Add the herb water and 2 teaspoons of the cooked herbs to the tomato mixture. (Discard the remaining cooked herbs.) Bring to a rapid boil. Add the pectin and boil rapidly for 1 minute.
3. Remove from heat and skim off the foam. Fill hot, sterilized (boiled 5 minutes in water to cover) half-pint jars with two-piece lids with the tomato mixture, leaving a ¼-inch headspace. Seal and process for 5 minutes in a boiling water bath.

6–8 HALF-PINT JARS

Marjoram symbolizes joy and is associated with young love.

Rutabaga Marmalade

A rutabaga by any other name is a turnip: a large, yellow, edible tuber. It seems an unlikely candidate for a sweet preserve, but here it is.

> 2 pounds rutabaga, peeled and chopped (5 cups)
> 5 oranges, chopped with peels on
> Juice of 3 lemons
> 5 cups sugar
> 1 cup water
> 1 teaspoon finely chopped fresh thyme or ⅓ teaspoon dried

Simmer the rutabaga for 5 minutes until tender but still firm. Drain. Combine with the oranges, lemon juice, sugar, water, and thyme. Cook over high heat, stirring frequently until syrup begins to jell. Overcooking will result in a mixture that is too thick.

Ladle into canning jars with two-piece lids, seal, and process in boiling water bath for 5 minutes.

5 HALF-PINT JARS

Thyme is symbolic of strength and courage.

Lemon Balm Lemonade

A little extra tang is added to old-fashioned lemonade with the addition of lemon balm. For those who want the shortcut, make the herb infusion and add it to frozen concentrate.

> 4 lemons, scrubbed
> Small bunch of lemon balm (about 3 ounces)
> ½ cup sugar
> ⅔ cup boiling water
> 2½ cups water
> Extra lemon balm sprigs for garnishing

1. Peel off the rinds of the lemons, avoiding the white part. Put the rinds in a small bowl. Tear off the lemon balm leaves and add them to the rinds. Add the sugar. Pour in the boiling water and stir well, crushing the leaves to release their flavor. Let this mixture stand for about 15 minutes.
2. Cut the lemons in half and squeeze out the juice. Put a few fresh sprigs of lemon balm into a large glass pitcher, then strain the lemon juice into it and add the cooled, strained syrup. Add the rest of the water, or half water and half ice cubes, and chill.

1 QUART

Mint Juleps

The classic drink of the South, a mint julep evokes images of antebellum ladies on wide verandas and gentlemen paying them calls. In reality, it's a potent drink with a sweet, minty chill. For the best effect, put glasses in the freezer long enough to frost them.

> 1 teaspoon sugar
> 1½ ounces bourbon
> 3 sprigs of mint
> Splash of soda water
> 1 paper-thin slice of lime

1. Combine the soda water, sugar, and 2 of the mint sprigs.
2. Pour the bourbon into a 10-ounce glass that has been filled with finely crushed ice.
3. Add the soda water, sugar, and mint mixture. Decorate with a sprig of mint and the slice of lime.

1 SERVING

Index

Converting Recipe Measurements to Metric

Use the following formulas for converting U.S. measurements to metric. Since the conversions are not exact, it's important to convert the measurements for all of the ingredients to maintain the same proportions as the original recipe.

WHEN THE MEASUREMENT GIVEN IS	MULTIPLY IT BY	TO CONVERT TO
teaspoons	4.93	milliliters
tablespoons	14.79	milliliters
fluid ounces	29.57	milliliters
cups (liquid)	236.59	milliliters
cups (liquid)	.236	liters
cups (dry)	275.31	milliliters
cups (dry)	.275	liters
pints (liquid)	473.18	milliliters
pints (liquid)	.473	liters
pints (dry)	550.61	milliliters
pints (dry)	.551	liters
quarts (liquid)	946.36	milliliters
quarts (liquid)	.946	liters
quarts (dry)	1101.22	milliliters
quarts (dry)	1.101	liters
gallons	3.785	liters
ounces	28.35	grams
pounds	.454	kilograms
inches	2.54	centimeters
degrees Fahrenheit (Centigrade)	$\frac{5}{9}$ (temperature $-$ 32)	degrees Celsius

While standard metric measurements for dry ingredients are given as units of mass, U.S. measurements are given as units of volume. Therefore, the conversions listed above for dry ingredients are given in the metric equivalent of volume.